Christmas
Naturals

Ornaments, Wreaths &
Decorations

Christmas
Naturals

Ornaments, Wreaths &
Decorations

CAROL TAYLOR

A Sterling/**Lark** Book
Sterling Publishing Co., Inc., New York

Art Director: Marcia Winters
Photography: Evan Bracken
Styling for location photography: Diane Weaver
Editorial assistance: Eric Carlson, Dawn Cusick
Production: Elaine Thompson and Sandra Montgomery

Library of Congress Cataloging in Publication Data
Taylor, Carol
    Christmas naturals : ornaments, wreaths & decorations /
  Carol Taylor.
    p.   cm.
  "A Sterling/Lark book."
  Includes bibliographical references and index.
  ISBN 0-8069-8360-4
  1. Christmas decorations.   2. Nature craft. I. Title
  TT900.C4T39   1991
  745.594'12–dc20   91-17552
                                                        CIP

ISBN 0-8069-8360-4

10 9 8 7 6 5 4 3 2 1

A Sterling/Lark Book

Produced by Altamont Press, Inc.
50 College St., Asheville, NC 28801

Published in 1991 by Sterling Publishing Co., Inc.
387 Park Ave. S., New York, NY 10016

Printed in Hong Kong by Oceanic Graphic Printing

Distributed in Canada by Sterling Publishing,
c/o Canadian Manda Group, P.O. Box 920, Station U, Toronto,
   Ontario M8Z 5P9
Distributed in the United Kingdom by Cassell PLC, Villers House,
   41/47 Strand, London WC2N 5JE, England
Distributed in Australia by Capricorn, Ltd., P.O. Box 665,
   Lane Cove, NSW 2066

CONTENTS

INTRODUCTION

Of all the small ceremonies that make up a Christmas season, my favorite is the first one: unpacking the decorations.

Each December the members of my household go about their business, ignoring the green tinsel sprouting from the street lights and the carols yodeling through the stores. We wait for some inner clock to tell us when the season has arrived. Finally, someone says, "Wanna unpack the decorations?"

Yes! We grab a ladder and head for the hall closet, where whoever is feeling brave teeters on the highest rung and hands down the familiar boxes. One by one we unwrap the bells and wreaths and ornaments, remembering who gave us this, where we bought that, taking affectionate inventory of our friends, our family, and the Christmases we have spent together.

Then it's Christmas.

Making Your Own

In almost every household, the homemade decorations are the most fun to unpack. If we made them ourselves, they remind us of the evenings we spent up to our elbows in artemisia and glue. If they were gifts, they remind us of the giver—and of that little catch of breath ("You made this for me?") when someone makes us a present of their time and their creativity.

Making Christmas decorations isn't difficult. You don't need advanced degrees or special powers—just a few tools and materials, a couple of evenings, and a conviction that in the vast territory between "perfect" and "ugly," there's lots of room to maneuver.

Using Natural Materials

In this book, "natural materials"

are plants or parts of plants: flowers and herbs both fresh and dried; evergreens and cones; spices and fruit; pods, seeds, grasses, and weeds. Some are cultivated. Others grow by the road, in the fields, or in the woods.

Working with natural materials changes the way you see. What used to look like scraggly brown weeds by the roadside, sad mementos of summer, now look like tall, graceful grasses with subtle colors and intricate shapes—perfect for a dried arrangement. You no longer wish someone would mow them down. You pick them instead.

Naturals can go rustic or elegant, and they can mix with glitzy accents without being outclassed. Wood mushrooms can hold their own with velvet ribbon. Deer moss is at least as well designed as gold mesh. You have only to glimpse a cluster of dry goldenrod backlit by the slanting winter sunlight to believe that natural materials are anything but shabby.

Where to Find Natural Materials

Craft stores. Most carry a fine selection of dried materials, some dyed, some left their natural color.

Florists. They stock up for Christmas with fresh and dried materials, some of which they'll sell you un-arranged.

Grocery stores. Many moderate-size supermarkets carry fresh flowers at reasonable prices. All have fresh fruit—apples, tangerines, pineapples, and grapes that are just as decorative as they are tasty. Keep an eye out for dried mushrooms, peppers, decorative gourds, and other interesting produce.

Backyard gardens. With the growing popularity of homemade wreaths and arrangements, all major seed companies carry such standards as artemisia,

celosia, lavender, globe amaranth, and gypsophila (baby's breath). The seeds will do you no good this year but can make next year's decorations lavish.

Import marts. These are good sources of eucalyptus and dried grasses.

The world at large. In this book you'll find sumac heads cut behind a commercial car wash, moss gathered in a backyard, rabbit tobacco picked along an interstate highway, pine cones rescued from a restaurant parking lot, and rose hips gathered from a pasture hedgerow. Weeds are everywhere.

Harvesting Natural Materials

Once you begin to notice (and covet) natural materials, you may discover some new truths about yourself—not all of them pretty. I recently found myself eyeing some spectacular red berries by my bank's front door and wondering whether the bank manager would really mind if I "pruned" the bushes. Just as I was taking careful note of closing hours, I remembered the basic rules of courtesy in the field.

■ Before you pick on private property, ask. For all you know, the owner of that car wash cherishes those sumac heads and will be seri-

ously displeased to discover you making off with them. Most of the time, people will be baffled that you even want their weeds and will enjoy being generous, but it's wise to check first.

■ Don't pick so much of anything that it can't come back next year. Rather than gathering all your ground pine from one patch, spread your picking out, taking a sprig here and there over a wide area.

■ Don't gather in public parks or campgrounds.

■ It almost (but not quite) goes without saying that if a plant is endangered, it should not be gathered at all. When posted signs plead with you to leave the sea oats on this particular beach, no ornament is worth it. The world is full (so far) of beautiful plants. After a momentary regret, you won't really miss this one.

How to Use This Book

Many of the projects in this book are the work of professional designers. Others are by enthusiastic amateurs. If a project suits you exactly, there's no reason not to duplicate it. Better yet, use the projects and the accompanying instructions for ideas and inspiration, then make something uniquely your own. And don't be deterred if some of the materials on any one project aren't readily at hand. If the globe amaranth crop was bad this year, substitute something else. If Fraser fir doesn't grow in your region, another greenery does—equally attractive, equally accessible.

Permission

One final caution: If you've always assumed that making Christmas decorations was something other people did—people with some mysterious talent you didn't possess— you may act a tad silly this year.

Let's say that your first project is a garland of boxwood and baby's breath, that it encircles the picture window in your living room, and that it's the single most gorgeous thing you've ever seen. You can't believe you made it. Fourteen times a day, you pass through the room, stop dead, and stare, with complete, unabashed admiration.

Eventually, you try to get a grip on yourself. Listen, you say, I've raised five children, I won the Nobel Prize in subatomic physics, I've lost four pounds. Why should I be so fatuously proud of one Christmas garland?

I don't know either. But it's okay. And if you'll show me yours, I'll show you mine.

CONTRIBUTING DESIGNERS

Julianne Bronder is a designer for Vans Floral Products in Alsip, Illinois. She studied at the American Floral Art School in Chicago and has taught floral design. (Pages 34, 46, 48, 49, 97, 108, 109, 112, and 113.)

Janet Frye owns The Enchanted Florist in Arden, North Carolina. Trained at Adam Eden Florist in Palm Springs, California, Janet has been a floral designer for 14 years and has taught design for seven. (Pages 17, 30, 31, 36, 37, 54, 55, 58, 64, 114, and 115.)

Fred Tyson Gaylor is a product designer at Hanford's, Inc., a wholesale holiday accessory company in Charlotte, North Carolina. He taught art in the public school for 10 years. (Pages 38, 100, 106, and 110.)

Cynthia Gilooley owns The Golden Cricket, a floral design studio in Asheville, North Carolina, where she enjoys whipping up slightly unconventional creations. (Pages 39 bottom, 43, 47, 56, and 60.)

Jeannette Hafner grows the flowers and greenery for her designs in her gardens in Orange, Connecticut. She teaches drying and arranging techniques as well as design classes. (Pages 69, 70, 71, 72, 73 top, 98, 99, 120, and 121.)

Carol Heller is a banker who resides in Durham, Connecticut, and enjoys designing with natural materials. (Pages 122, 123, 124, 125, and 127.)

Wana Henry, a craftsperson from Church Hill, Tennessee, works primarily with cones and seeds, and markets her work at craft fairs. (Pages 35 bottom, 79, 90, 91, and 93 bottom.)

Judy Horn specializes in corn husk crafts. With husband Dave, she owns The Corn Husk Shoppe in Weaverville, North Carolina, where she sells her corn husk flowers and dolls, along with wreaths and arrangements. (Pages 40, 41, 102, 103, and 107.)

Alyce Nadeau grows 200 different herbs for her business, Goldenrod Mountain Herbs, in Deep Gap, North Carolina. She designs a wide range of herbal items and has been known to arrange an herbal wedding, complete with food, beverage, and bouquets. (Pages 32, 68, 73 bottom, 74, 75, 80, 86, 87, 88, 89, and 126.)

Alan Salmon and **Betty Sparrow** own and operate Wildwood Herbal Flower Farm at Reems Creek, in Weaverville, North Carolina. They sell fresh and dried herbs and flowers, along with wreaths, bouquets, and flower baskets.

For the projects on pages 81 and 84, they enlisted the help of Alan's sister, Jeanne Whitaker. (The front cover and pages 35 top, 81, and 84.)

Sandy Mush Herb Nursery, Leicester, North Carolina, is the full-time passion of the Jayne family. They grow an extensive variety of culinary, decorative, and fragrant herbs, which they sell, along with their wreaths, through their mail-order catalogs. (Pages 39 top, 61, 62, 63, 85, 92 inset, 96, 111, 117, and 119.)

Diane Weaver worked as an art director/designer in Detroit and New York. With husband Dick, she operates Gourmet Gardens, an herb nursery in Weaverville, North Carolina. She uses some of the 180 herbs they grow to design and make wreaths, arrangements, culinary herb mixtures, and herb butters. (Pages 26, 28, 42, 44, 50, 52, 65, 66, 67, 76, 77, 78, 94, 104, 116, and 118.)

And thanks to . . .
Pat Barnes (pages 59, 92, and 93 top), Darlene Conti (82 and 83), Rasland Farms (33), Sarah Searcy (8 and 60), and Elly Shriver (128).

TOOLS & MATERIALS

GLUE GUNS

A glue gun may not be the most fun you can have for under $10, but it's close. Fast, easy to use, and incredibly flexible, it will affix almost anything to almost anything else.

For this book, designers used glue guns to attach flowers, herbs, cones, nuts, seeds, pods, bows, ribbons, lace, twigs, vines, lichens, and birds (fake, of course) to bases of foam, moss, vine, straw, and plastic.

To use a glue gun, simply insert a glue stick, plug in the gun, and wait for it to heat. Then aim and squeeze the trigger. Hold the glued items together for half a minute or so, until the bond is firm.

A few tips:

■ Cover the work area with newspaper. Almost all glue guns drip.

■ A glue gun that can stand up when you set it down is extremely convenient. When shopping for a gun, check to see whether it has a stand in front (some are detachable and included in the box) and whether the handle is designed to sit flat, increasing its stability and reducing the number of times you'll knock it over. If the gun has no stand, rest it on a ceramic plate or some other fireproof container between shots.

■ As you work, the gun will produce ethereal strands of glue that resemble spiderwebs. Just remember to pull them off the project when you're done.

■ If you're working with a plastic foam base, test a small area first. Almost all guns will melt foam, but some cause more damage than others. If a deep, moist crater appears on the base, cover it with moss, using floral greening pins. Then glue your materials to the moss.

■ Don't hesitate to use as much glue as you need. Many times a small dab will suffice, but some of the refined-looking projects in later chapters conceal globs of glue the size of calamata olives.

■ Anything that will melt foam can burn fingers; exercise some care. If you find that you burn yourself frequently, investigate the "warm melt" guns on the market. They use glue sticks that melt at a lower temperature and thus don't get as hot.

■ Unplug the gun as soon as you're finished, and never leave an unsupervised child around a gun.

FLORAL FOAM

Foam allows you to convert a pile of flowers into an arrangement and a bag of fruit into a wreath—in other words, the parts into a whole. Since foam isn't nearly as pretty as it is useful, it's at its best covered with greenery or flowers, providing an invisible means of support.

Foam comes in two forms: dry and wet. Each has advantages.

Dry. This is the rigid plastic foam (Styrofoam, for example) readily available in craft shops, discount houses, and department stores. It comes in a variety of shapes—sheets, cones, balls, squares, and rectangles—and is easily cut and shaped even further with a serrated knife.

It also comes in white or green. Given a choice, use whichever color blends best with the materials you're attaching (for example, a green foam base for an herbal wreath). That way, if a section does manage to peek through, it is less glaring.

Some blocks of foam come with a self-adhesive strip on the bottom, convenient for securing to a container—for example, the bowl that will hold an arrangement. If there's

no strip, there's no problem. Floral tape, clay, or wire, a glue gun, or brute force will all work well.

Evergreens and flowers with tough stems can be inserted directly into the foam; just cut the stem at an angle to provide a pointed end. Weak-stemmed flowers must be attached to floral picks and then inserted (see page 12).

Wet. This fine-grained floral foam (touch it, and a fine dust comes off on your fingers) is invaluable for fresh arrangements. When soaked in water, it will absorb and hold moisture for weeks. Thus, fresh materials inserted into it can absorb moisture as they need it. Wet foam allows you to decorate a tabletop Christmas tree, for example, with fresh carnations (page 115) that will last through the season.

Wet-type foam comes in "bricks" like the one at the bottom left corner of the page.

Occasionally, designers use dry foam without wetting it, when they're working with especially delicate dried flowers, when they want an especially small piece of foam, or when there's nothing else around the house.

PICKS

A floral pick looks like an overgrown toothpick with a piece of thin, flexible wire attached to one end. Picks come in various sizes, most typically three inches or six inches long (7.5 or 15 cm.). They're available in unfinished wood or painted green, the latter being less visible in a thicket of foliage, and in craft shops and discount marts. A pick acts as an artificial stem. Its sharp end penetrates a variety of bases—foam, straw, and (less successfully) vine—and holds upright and stable whatever flimsy plant or odd-shaped item is attached to it. In a vine base, a pick must be reinforced with hot glue. Otherwise, either it won't go in far enough or it wobbles around in the spaces between the coiled vines.

Materials can be attached to a pick by wire, glue, or simple jabbing. For wiring, hold the pick and a plant's stem together, making sure that whatever you want to be visible—the flower, the best greenery—is above the pick's wire. Tightly wrap the wire around both the stem and the pick, starting with several horizontal turns at the top and then spiraling down the length of the stem. You might want to snip off the stem if it extends beyond the pick, for easier insertion into the base.

For a more durable result, wrap the wired pick and stem with floral tape—just stretch and wrap. With this final step, the stem is less likely to be dislodged.

Follow a similar procedure for a small bunch of flowers or greenery. Arrange them into the bouquet you want, wrap the wire around the pick and all the stems, and finish off with floral tape.

If an object (a sturdy mushroom, for example) has nothing long, thin, and vertical to wire the pick to, you can hot-glue it to the top of the pick and go from there. In a pinch, you can even jam the top of the pick into an expendable item—for example, an apple or a tangerine—and call it art.

PINS

Floral pins—also known as "fern pins" or "greening pins"—are quick and easy to use. They will attach bunches of herbs or flowers to a straw base and moss of all sorts to a foam one, a task at which they excel.

A moss-covered base can be an integral part of the design—see the luxuriant wreath on page 30—or merely an insurance policy. Many designers cover a foam base with moss before adding any other materials, so that if the base accidentally peeks through, the viewer will see natural moss rather than naked foam. (The block of foam below is invisible under curly Spanish moss, which is attached with an equally invisible pin.) Moreover, it's often easier to hot-glue materials to moss than to meltable foam.

WIRE

A cone, a bow, even a bunch of grapes can be attached to a base with a piece of wire. Although common hardware-variety wire will work, floral wire—inexpensive, flexible, and green—is well worth a trip to your neighborhood craft shop or discount store. It comes in several thicknesses, or gauges, all of which are useful on various occasions. Attaching a small cone calls for the thinnest, most flexible wire you can find; forming the "spine" of a garland demands a heavy-duty gauge.

Wiring is especially useful on wreaths, since the base is a convenient diameter for wrapping wire around. A vine base is perfect; each coil of vine provides a point of purchase.

To wire an object, first look it over for an inconspicuous place to attach the wire. If there is none, plan to hide the wire later with other materials —a sprig of greenery, perhaps.

Fold a length of wire loosely in half and slip it around the object, with the ends of wire on the back side. Twist the strands of wire together, right next to the item, so that the object is held securely. Now hold it tightly against the base, with the two wires straddling the base. Again twist the strands until the object is held firmly in place. Reinforce with hot glue if necessary.

An especially delicate item— a small cone, for instance—may fare better if you carefully loop the end of the wire around it, leaving yourself a single long stem to wrap around (or insert into) the base.

To wire a piece of fruit—a lemon or tangerine, for example— pierce it with a heavy-gauge wire end-to-end, and wrap the ends of the wire around the base.

MAKING WREATHS

Some people are born with nimble fingers, muscular egos, and a natural affinity for crafts. Then there's the rest of us, who remain dubious about the whole business well into adulthood. For us, a wreath is often our first craft project.

It finally dawns on us that anybody—anybody—can wind a red ribbon around a straw base, insert a few sprigs of greenery and some silver bells, and hang on the front door a decoration that we made, by George, ourselves.

After that first confidence-building wreath, we branch out into other bases, other means of attachment, other materials, other locations, and, frequently, other crafts.

Bases. Even small crafts stores stock a variety of wreath bases: straw, moss, vine, foam, wire, paper, even rattan. In December, foam bases covered with ground cinnamon appear in some craft shops. Sizes range from tiny to huge.

Attachment. Gluing, picking, wiring, pinning—all are legitimate means of getting natural materials to stay where you want them.

Materials. Evergreens, flowers fresh or dried, berries, cones, fruit, nuts, seedheads, pods—if it's pretty enough for you to lean down and pick up, it's wreath material. (Assuming, of course, reasonable size and weight. Fenceposts are probably out.)

Locations. Wreaths have traditionally graced front doors and mantlepieces, but they also look good elsewhere: interior doors, walls, windows, cabinets, and every room of the house, even the bath.

An outside wreath invites your guests inside, whether it's hanging on an exterior wall, a gatepost, a lamppost, or even a tree close to the house.

Tips
All of these suggestions for applying materials are violated regularly and deliberately, with splendid results. But they're still good general rules.

■ Start with your background material—something you have lots of, which covers well, and which you like (it will be prominent in the wreath). Possibilities include moss (see page 30), silver king artemisia (page 35), boxwood (page 26), bay leaves (page 44), and sorghum heads (page 37).
■ Usually, materials should be inserted into the base at the same angle. In the wreath on page 34, for example, carefully angled eucalyptus sprigs produce a pinwheel effect.
■ Framing the outside of the wreath can be effective. For example, on page 47 magnolia leaves encircle the wreath, providing a frame for the apples and grapes.
■ If the base is attractive, part of it—even most of it—can be left bare. Vine bases are interesting and complex, either natural (page 43) or misted with paint (page 39), and pine needle bases are attractively rough and rustic (page 40).

But bare sections need to be deliberate. Unintended bare patches will spoil a wreath. In applying background material, overlap the picked or wired bunches as you go around the wreath, thus covering the base thoroughly.

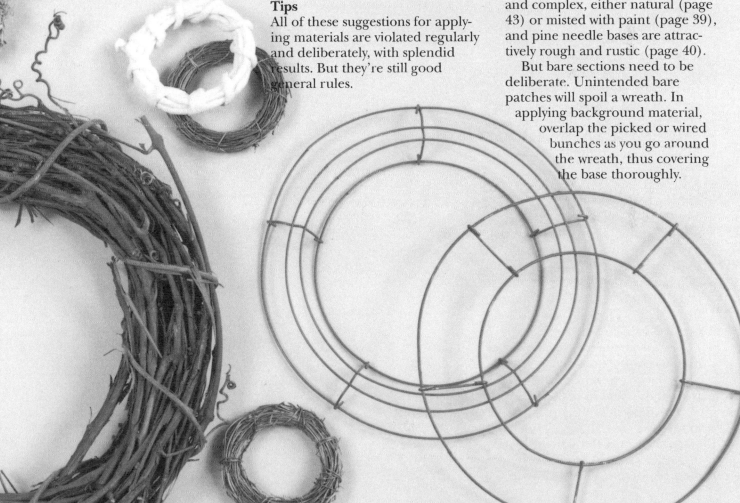

MAKING ARRANGEMENTS

Foam. Choose either dry foam, for dried arrangements, or wet foam, for fresh materials, and cut it to fit the container. Make sure the foam is taller than the sides of the bowl, so that you can insert materials into it horizontally. For extra security, tape the foam to the pot.

(Some stores carry a type of floral tape made especially for wet form.)

Container. As long as it's stable and will hold a piece of foam large enough to support all the materials you plan to use, the container can be just about anything: vase, flowerpot, pitcher, bowl. Reconnoiter your cupboard. You may find favorite pieces that can be brought out of the closet and used.

Sometimes a container-within-a-container is the solution. Baskets make handsome holders for natural materials, but they're often too large and oddly shaped to fill with foam, always too leaky and easily water-stained to hold fresh flowers. Place a piece of foam in a bowl, the bowl in the basket, and crumpled newspaper around the sides, to hold the bowl in place.

The designer of the partridge in the pear tree on page 110 wanted to hold a tree branch upright in plaster of Paris, but he certainly didn't want to harden plaster in a good brass urn. So he poured the plaster into a cheap plastic pot, placed that inside the urn, and saved his brass.

Shape. An arrangement needs an overall shape: triangular, for example, or oval, or round. Whether you make yours vertical or horizonal may depend on where you intend to display it. For example, the horizontal arrangement on page 52 echoes the lines of the table it sits on.

The overall shape may be defined completely by the materials themselves, or the eye may be allowed to fill in the gaps. The triangle on page 59 is unmistakable; every inch of it is filled with plants. But the arrangement on page 58 is also triangular. Between the tip of the taller candle and the tips of the cedar branches on each side there's nothing much but air. Still, those three points form the perimeter of the arrangement, and the eye connects them—one reason this arrangement is so satisfying.

Color. When most of us look at grapes, red onions, and orchids, we see fruit, vegetables, and flowers. One designer looked at them and saw purple—which is how they all ended up in the arrangement on page 56.

As you look for natural materials, try defining them, not in the usual way, but as colors. You may find that you quite literally see things differently, and stumble upon materials you would otherwise never have thought to use.

Application. Generally, it's useful to establish the boundaries of the

arrangement first—to insert the flower or greenery that will provide the highest point, then the materials that will define the outside diameter. With the general shape to guide you, go back and fill in the arrangement.

It's also useful to apply heavy or bulky materials before light, delicate ones. For one thing, the materials are less likely to be damaged that way.

In the arrangement pictured, the designer first inserted the carnations (the highest one first) into the wet foam. With the perimeters drawn, she filled in with bulky galax leaves, then with poms, and, finally, with featherweight spengeri fern.

Focal point. Many arrangements have one component so eye-catching that it inevitably be-

comes the focal point of the arrangement—all eyes immediately focus on it. If you plan to use a showy bow, for example, or a large, spectacular flower, give some thought to exactly where it should be.

Angle. Consider the height at which the arrangement will be displayed—a high mantelpiece, a low coffee table, a waist-high sideboard—and work on it at that angle. Otherwise, no one may see its best side.

Candles. Metal or plastic candle holders are widely available, ready to insert into the base. Another option is to tape two floral picks to the candle. Not only is a picked candle more stable, but the base takes up less room in the arrangement.

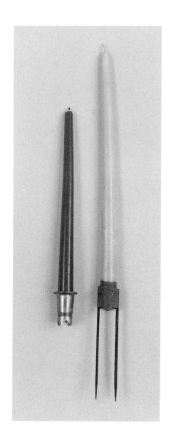

MAKING GARLANDS

Perhaps it's all those Victorian woodcuts of merrymakers in long gowns and frock coats, draping greenery down a banister. Whatever the reason, when we plan to deck the halls, we think inevitably of garlands.

Making a garland entails attaching decorative materials to a long "spine"—something thin, flexible, and tough.

Most children have strung cranberries for the tree, using ordinary needle and thread. That's a garland, and it can be combined with others and used other places (see page 104). Variations abound. Tough little globe amaranth blossoms can be strung the same way, for a brilliant result (page 84), as can anything else that's sturdy enough to be pierced without falling apart.

If you're dealing with materials that are not conveniently round, you'll need a different spine and a different means of attachment.

Heavy-gauge wire makes a good, durable spine, but the favorite of many designers is jute cord—the type used for macrame. Cut the cord a little longer than you want the garland to be. Some people tie it between two supports—two chair backs, for example—at a comfortable working height; others prefer a work table or the floor.

Wherever you choose to work, form a small bunch of greenery and/or flowers (half a dozen stems or so) and wire the stems together. Then wire the bunch to the spine, using fine, spool-type floral wire. Then wire on another bunch, over-lapping the previous one. Continue down the length of the cord, until the garland is finished.

The artistry comes in the composition of the bunches. You can make bunches of individual materials and alternate them down the garland—one bunch of Fraser fir, then one of blue spruce, then gypsophila, then repeat—or each bunch can be composed of several different materials.

After the garland is complete, decorative accents—berries, Christmas balls, knickknacks—can be hot-glued in place. A bow can be wired at either end, at the center, or both.

MAKING SWAGS

Broadly defined, swags are bouquets designed to hang—on a wall, a door, a chimney, a cabinet. They can range from beautifully simple to strikingly complex.

Vertical bouquets. The simplest swag consists of greenery or flowers wired together by the stems, usually with a bow wired on to cover the attached stems. Since the design is predictable, all attention focuses on the materials, which need to be very attractive if this decoration is to work. The traditional swag on page 97, for example, displays very fresh, very colorful Christmas greenery to good advantage.

Horizontal bouquets. Not just bouquets hung by their "ankles," horizonal swags are somewhat more complicated to make (but not much). Usually, background material—for example, the ever-popular silver king artemisia on page 98—is divided into two bunches, which are placed end to end, with their foliage to the right and left, their stems in the center. With these stems overlapped and wired together, additional materials are wired or hot-glued on, radiating from the center and following the basic shape. A bow wired in the center hides the wired stems.

Backing. A third type of swag consists of materials attached to a solid backing that gives the decoration shape. The heavy door swag on page 106 has a backing of foam glued onto a board.

Found objects. Some of the most intriguing swags consist of an object decorated with natural materials. Anything interesting will serve: a cinnamon broom (page 107), a garlic braid (page 94), even an antique sickle (page 109). This is perhaps the most imagination-stretching swag to put together: spotting an everyday object that, with a little dressing up, is worth displaying.

MAKING TREES

Poet Joyce Kilmer wrote that "only God can make a tree," but then he'd never heard of Styrofoam. If you're trying for only a tabletop model, you have lots of options.

Vine. Vine trees are widely available in craft stores or Christmas shops, ready to be decorated to your taste. Or you can make your own. Gather a good quantity of thin, dried vines—honeysuckle, grapevine, wisteria, whatever grows where you are. (Note: If you're allergic to poison ivy or oak, you will react to the dry vines as you do to the green leaves. It's wise to know what you're getting into.) Another option is to buy a vine wreath and uncurl it.

However you get them, soak the vines for four or five hours, to soften them. Make a cone-shaped cardboard form, and wrap the pliable vines around it. Allow to dry overnight, and remove the tree from its form.

Foam. Plastic foam cones, widely available, supply ready-made tree shapes. They're stable enough to stand upright on their own, and materials can be inserted or picked directly into them, following the basic tree shape. The one shown has boxwood stems inserted into the top and a piece of ground

pine picked into the bottom. A cone can also be glued to the end of an upright tree branch for a Douglas fir shape (see page 110, for example).

A brick of wet floral foam, stood on end, makes a good base for a tree that includes fresh materials. Tape the foam securely to a shallow container, making the tape bite into the foam, and insert materials so that they form a tree shape. Water the tree from the top, for a long-lasting decoration.

Foam balls are also useful for a topiary style of tree. Hot-glued to the top of a tree branch, they can make an interesting double tree (see page 112).

Faux tree. (Please. Not "artificial," but "faux." You may be faking it, but you're faking it with class.) A green plastic tree looks undeniably fake, but if it's covered with natural materials, no one will know. (Check out pages 120 and 121, and be honest; could you tell?) Faux trees are so inexpensive and convenient that even the most committed naturalists buy them and hot-glue natural materials onto them.

Plants. Live plants that are naturally tree-shaped—or can be pruned that way—make interesting table trees. A cactus, for example, or a rosemary plant (page 116) can turn into a Christmas tree overnight.

MAKING ORNAMENTS

An ornament can be a single interesting item—for example, a milkweed pod—attached to an ornament hanger with a dab of hot glue. It can be a small bunch of berries, dried flowers, or grasses tied with ribbon. It can be a foam or glass ball with natural materials glued onto it.

Walk around your yard, wander through the woods, and scan the roadsides as you drive, redefining what you see. Is that a Christmas ornament that no one else has recognized?

Then head for the crafts store, scanning not just the Christmas section but other areas as well. Small baskets offer endless possibilities, as do other miniature containers (flowerpots, toy watering cans, wheelbarrows, kitchen implements). The dried materials are worth considering: a lotus pod makes an interesting ornament (see page 89).

Tips

■ Think light. An ornament doesn't have to be very heavy at all to make a fir branch as droopy as the post-Christmas blues.

■ Keep in mind that the ornament will be displayed on a green tree. Unless the observer is very close indeed, or the texture is markedly different, greenery on an ornament won't show up.

■ Be sure to attach the hanger (whether ribbon or wire) so that the ornament will hang with the correct side out. Since tree branches usually project out from the center of the tree, most hangers should go from side to side, rather than from front to back.

■ An excellent hanger for foam balls is a "hairpin" made of heavy-gauge floral wire, stuck into the ball. A commercial wire hanger can attach to that.

DECORATING PACKAGES

A present that is hand-decorated with natural materials sends a special warmth. It makes a gift, not only of the contents, but of your time and creativity as well.

To create distinctive packages, you'll need only natural materials and a glue gun. After wrapping the package with paper in the normal fashion, position the materials in a pleasing arrangement, and hot-glue them to the paper or to each other. If desired, add a bow or mix in some artificial fruit, berries, or a small bird.

Tips

■ Consider the package as a whole: the paper, the natural materials, and (if you're using one) the ribbon. Make sure the colors of paper and the naturals complement each other.

■ When selecting natural materials, try for a variety of shapes and textures. On the package below, fuzzy strawflowers and rigid pine cones provide contrasting textures.

■ Arrange the natural materials in an identifiable shape—a crescent, circle, or rectangle, for example. It helps to do a few dry runs, laying out the materials in a variety of combinations on a scrap of paper before actually gluing them down.

■ Start with relatively flat background materials, then add the more three-dimensional items.

■ Packages can be wrapped in fabric, rather than paper, with natural materials hot-glued on in the same fashion—often with memorable results.

MAKING CORN HUSK FLOWERS

The cinnamon-broom swag on page 107 and the wreaths on pages 40 and 41 get part of their charm from corn husk flowers. The blooms may look complicated, but they're not difficult to make.

Corn husks can be purchased at craft stores or shucked from actual ears of corn. If you peel your own, be careful not to tear the husks as you remove them; the larger the husks, the easier they are to work with. Spread them in the sun to dry, keeping them in a thin layer and turning them often, so they'll dry quickly without mildew.

If you want colored flowers, fabric dyes work well on corn husks. Dissolve approximately half a package of dye in half a gallon of water, and heat to boiling. (Actual amounts can vary with the stiffness of the husks and the amount of natural yellow they have.) Dip the husks in the hot dye. If you want a deep hue, remove the dye from the heat and let the husks soak overnight.

Looped Flowers

1. Tear your stiffest husks lengthwise into strips. You'll need five strips about 1-3/4 inches (4.4 cm.) wide for the petals.

2. Use your less attractive husks to make the center. Roll the husks into a roll about 3/4 inch in diameter, and wire with firm wire about an inch (2.5 cm.) from the top. Trim the wire ends and excess corn husk, leaving about an inch of husk below the wire.

3. Fold the petal strips in half and position them around the center. Wire them to the center either one by one or all at once, whichever is easier.

4. Trim excess husks from the bottom, tapering the base instead of cutting straight across.

5. Cut a piece of heavy wire about 18 inches (45 cm.) long. Make a "fish hook" in one end and insert the other end into the center. Carefully pull the wire down through the flower until the hook anchors in the center. Tape the flower to the wire with masking tape, covering the flower's tapered base and about 1/2 inch (1.25 cm.) of the wire. Wrap the base and the entire stem with floral tape. (See the shaggy flower below.)

Shaggy Flowers

1. Gather pieces of husk in a bundle, with the natural points in the same direction. The fatter the bundle, the larger the flower. A good working diameter is two inches (5 cm.).

2. Wire the bundle tightly with heavy floral wire about 5-1/2 inches (13.75 cm.) from the top (the pointed ends), and trim off excess husk, tapering the cut.

3. Tear the husks into large strips.

Or shred the husks with a hat pin, for a wispy, curly effect. Shredded husks will curl naturally as they continue to dry.

4. Add a stem as described for the looped flowers. The stem can remain beautifully long and straight, for arrangements, or twist around a wreath base for anchoring.

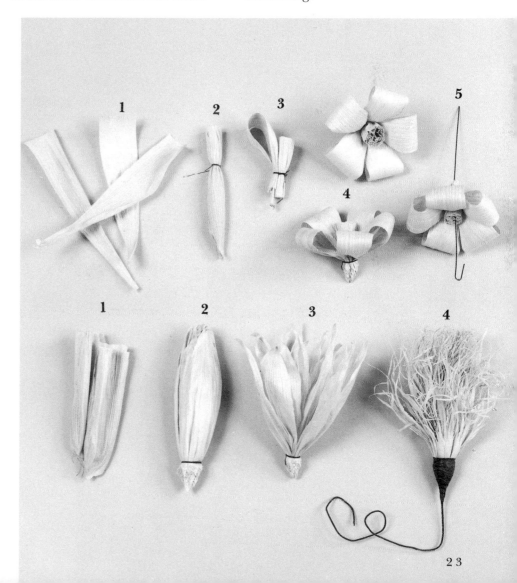

MAKING BOWS

To have tried to make a bow is to understand despair. The ribbon seems to take on a life (and a passive-aggressive personality) of its own, wriggling out of your fingers one moment, lying there limply the next. And it's small comfort that every smart-aleck you talk to says there's nothing to it.

There's nothing to it. Especially at Christmas, craft stores stock ready-made, red velvet bows in various sizes and will probably make you a bow of any ribbon in stock.

On the other hand, there are wonderful ribbons—watered silk, paper, raffia, taffeta, grosgrain, metallic, net, lace, velvet cord, satin tapestry—sold by places that do not make bows. If you do, you can turn a good project into a smashing one.

Picked Loops

An easy option is to wire loops of ribbon onto floral picks. Just fold a piece of ribbon loosely in half, pinch the ends together against a pick, and wrap the wire around the ribbon. The picked loops at the lower left of this page were made three different ways: with a tail, with two loops, and with a single loop.

To create a bow, pick the loops into the base of your project, one on top of the other. In the arrangement on page 54, the bow at the lower left consists of three picked loops.

Real Bows

1. Form a circle at the end of the ribbon. (The one in the photo is lying on its side.)

2. Pinch the circle together in the center, and hold it there. This is even easier than it sounds.

3. Adding to the back of the bow, form loops of ribbon, first on one side, then the other, continuing until the bow is as full as you want it. This is harder than it sounds.

4. Wire the bow together in the center, leaving long enough wire ends for attaching to the project.

5. Shape the bow, pulling the loops into position. Move a loop around by inserting your finger inside it and pulling; if you pinch the loop closed, it will flatten.

Tips

■ The key words are "pinch and twist."

As you complete each new loop by bringing the ribbon back to the center of the bow, pinch the ribbon in the middle and twist it, so that the upper side becomes the lower one. Otherwise, half of the loops will be wrong-side-out.

■ A bow wired onto a pick is often easier to insert in an arrangement or wreath.

■ Don't underestimate the amount of ribbon you'll need. A decent-sized bow can eat up four yards of ribbon without even trying.

■ Learning to make bows is largely a matter of fiddling with a ribbon until until you like the result, then repeating the process until you've got it down. It's not a bad way to spend a rainy afternoon.

This three-foot-long (90 cm.) wreath can decorate even the largest fireplace without looking skimpy. The base is heavy, galvanized clothesline wire shaped into an oval, with the ends overlapped about three inches (7.5 cm.) and taped together with duct tape. Bunches of boxwood—three or four branches about 12 inches (30 cm.) long wired together—were wired to the base, starting at the bottom and working up one side, overlapping the bunches to cover the stems of the previous bunch. The other side was then covered in a similar manner. Three-inch burgundy cockscomb heads were hot-glued close to the base of the boxwood bunches, using lots of glue. The rest of the materials were then hot-glued at random to the branches: white strawflowers, sprigs of baby's breath, red globe amaranth, and holly leaves that had been gilded with a paint pen. A bow made from three yards (2.8 m.) of wired burgundy ribbon was wired to the top of the wreath, and its streamers woven down the sides.

When the Christmas spirit strikes late, ready-made bases are invaluable time-savers. Embellished with natural materials, plain evergreen wreaths and garlands can become uniquely your own.

To make a wreath and garland like the ones shown, first prepare the flowers and fruit. Cut five three-inch (7.5 cm.) green foam balls in half, and hot-glue colorful flowers over the spherical sides. Six of those pictured are covered with globe amaranth; four, with celosia. Then wire the dried pomegranates: run a seven-inch (17.5 cm.) piece of wire through the center of each fruit, top to bottom. Make a fish hook on the bottom, and pull it back into the fruit, anchoring it firmly.

Wire a few sprigs of boxwood or other greenery around the wreath, for variety in the foliage. Wire the pomegranates to the wreath, and hot-glue on the flower-foam balls, spacing them evenly.

Make a bow with long streamers from four yards (3.7 m.) of wired net ribbon and wire it to the top, trailing the streamers around the wreath. Hot-glue sprigs of yarrow, clusters of pepperberries, and additional amaranth and celosia to the foliage.

Arrange the swag in position on the mantle, then attach the flowers. Pick small bunches of red-dyed bunnytails, globe amaranth, and celosia into the branches, and hot-glue sumac heads to the sides. Wire a bow to the center, and weave the ribbon ends in and out of the swag. Finally, hot-glue globe amaranth, peppers, yarrow, and zinnias over the entire swag.

30

LEFT: Be prepared: when you put velvety green moss on a wreath, people are going to fondle it. Fresh sheet moss covers this 14-inch (35 cm.) straw base, which the designer attached with floral pins. She then wired a small piece of rigid foam to the top, providing a point of purchase for flowers, and wrapped metallic-gold wired ribbon around the wreath, with the ends pinned in place. The same ribbon supplied a bow. (To curl the streamers, wrap the ribbon around a candle, a dowel, or your finger.) Flowers and berries are attached to the foam in a crescent shape: first the miniature myrtle and German statice, then rose hips, then dried asters and roses. Small accent pieces are hot-glued to the lower right.

BELOW: In late fall, rose hips still cling to the leafless branches of rose bushes, both tame and wild. They make colorful Christmas wreaths. For this one, the designer hot-glued branches of rose hips onto a vine base and then added small cedar tips, tucking them around and under the berries and attaching them with a glue gun. A scattering of cone "roses" finished the wreath.

If you can't lay your hands on any rose hips, bittersweet berries will also work. Just peel off the outer, gold-colored petal.

LEFT: All ready to hang on a headboard or bedroom wall, this graceful wreath has a grapevine base. After hot-gluing 10 sprigs of eucalyptus around the base at an angle, the designer made small bouquets of hydrangea by taping their stems together, and glued them around the base, carefully inserting the stems of the last bunch under the head of the first one. She then hot-glued a ribbon in loops around the outside, with each loop beginning and ending halfway between the eucalyptus sprigs. Sprigs of baby's breath hot-glued around the outside finished the wreath.

BELOW: Fragrant sweet Annie formed the base for this floral wreath. The greenery was wrapped around a wooden pegged frame, then removed from the frame and tied with floral wire. The dried flowers were affixed to the base with tacky glue: miniature roses, lavender, blue salvia, celosia, statice, strawflowers, and globe amaranth.

Long, striped protea pods steal the show in this mix of materials. The straw base is wrapped with strapping tape to provide extra support. Sprigs of eucalyptus, picked around the wreath at an angle, supply the background; picked okra and protea pods add interest. Protea foliage, German statice, and faux red berries, hot-glued around the wreath, add variety and color.

wreath shape makes a perfect base; just wire the cones, insert the wire ends into two adjacent holes, and twist. Hot-glue nuts around the wreath at attractive intervals.

Clip long wires on the back and attach a wire hanger. It's helpful to cover the back: cut out a "dough-nut" of felt and glue it on. The wreath can either hang on a wall or sit on a table, with a fat candle in the center.

LEFT: The scents of this herbal wreath linger on the air without overpowering all who come near. Small bunches of dried sage, mint, southernwood, and silver king artemisia were wired together, then pinned around a straw base with floral pins, with the bunches overlapping to cover the base. Accents of red peppers, globe amaranth, bittersweet berries, and yarrow were pinned among the herbs. Some of the yarrow was left its natural yellow; other was dyed a soft orange with fabric dye.

RIGHT: A study in brown, this cone-and-nut wreath displays the intricate patterns supplied by nature, that master designer.

Gather cones soon after they fall from the tree or simply pluck them off. Test by squeezing: if the cone doesn't crumble, it's usable. Nuts are equally variable: buckeyes, acorns, hazelnuts, even peach pits.

Bake all nuts for 25 minutes at 200° F., and clip any stems from cones. For variety in color, cones can be soaked in a strong bleach solution and allowed to dry. To make the flowers, cut cones care-fully crosswise and remove any seeds that spoil the shape.

A piece of pegboard cut into a

LEFT: Essential to southwestern cuisine, large red ancho peppers make an arresting Christmas wreath in any part of the country. The base for this one is a wire ring wrapped in raffia, which provides both a strong base and a wide, flat surface for attaching materials. All materials are hot-glued on, the peppers first, then the accents: miniature corn, eucalyptus sprigs, cone flowers, nuts, and pods. A wired raffia bow adds a final splash of color.

BELOW: Regardless of what else is in the room, this dramatic wreath will capture attention. For one thing, everyone will want to know what on earth it's made of. The answer: sorghum cane tops.

The designer wired sorghum tops onto a 16-inch (40 cm.) straw base, with each bunch overlapping the wired stems of the previous one. With the base completely covered, she sprayed it with a clear acrylic sealer, adding gloss and resilience. The next step was to wire on the bow, made from four yards (3.7 m.) of wired ribbon, in a watered-silk pattern. Then she hot-glued Christmas balls around the wreath, and glued cedar sprigs in place. Finally, she shaped the long ribbon streamers and glued them into position.

LEFT: Materials become traditional if they work so well we refuse to stop using them. The holly, pine, boxwood, and nandina berries in this Christmas wreath welcome all who approach the house.

To prolong the greenery's freshness, the designer cut it into short lengths and immersed it in water overnight. The next day, he picked small bunches around the outside edge of a straw base, starting at what would become the focal point—the bottom—and working up one side to the top, then working up the opposite side. Then he covered the rest of the base with greenery, picked in bunches of nandina berries, and wired a generous red bow to the bottom.

ABOVE: Sprigs of Fraser fir define the outside of this wreath, with bright green ground pine circling the center. White yarrow and pearly everlasting, reddish brown chamaecyparis, sweet Annie, and blue-green oregano provide colorful accents. All materials are picked into a straw base.

LEFT: If you mean to have a cotton-picking Christmas, here's the way to start. Mist a grapevine wreath with flat white paint from a spray can. Then wrap the wreath with narrow gold-metallic ribbon, and attach a few branches of cedar and a gold bow with hot glue. While the glue gun is still hot, attach the cotton bolls—full ones, half-open ones, and empty ones (those brown, starlike shapes). Then glue on a few sumac heads for extra color.

BELOW: Two red corn husk flowers and a lush green bow provide the focal point of this wreath. Pine needle bases such as this one are widely available, and corn husk flowers appear in some craft shops and specialty stores. (To make your own flowers, see page 23.) Attach the flowers first, by twisting their wire stems around the base. Make six or seven bows with three loops on each side, and nestle them around the flowers, twisting the wires around the base to attach them. Continue adding bows until the wreath is as full as you like. Finally, wrap a ribbon around the base and attach it with hot-glue.

RIGHT: Corn husk flowers, German statice, and red velvet ribbon make a memorable wreath. First attach the flowers by twisting their wire stems around the vine base. If necessary, secure them with additional wire. The flowers should be just touching; they can be gently pulled apart later to accommodate a bow. (To make your own corn husk flowers, see page 23.) Next, make nine or 10 bows, tuck them around the flowers, and wire them to the base. Continue to add bows until the wreath looks full enough. Hot-glue a piece of ribbon to the wreath and wrap it around the base. Finally, hot-glue pieces of German statice among the bows and down the base.

This striking ivory wreath illustrates just how many different shades come under the heading "white." The designer wired sphagnum moss around a six-inch (15 cm.) wire ring, to provide a pale, natural base. She then wired artemisia around the base, using very lightweight wire. The rest of the materials were hot-glued on: strawflowers, globe amaranth, white yarrow, baby's breath, and pearly everlasting.

This small wreath could grace a cabinet front, a bedstead, or a dark-colored wall. It is shown wired to a green silk hatbox, where it seems to shimmer.

This jaunty wreath combines natural and faux materials, all hotglued onto a grapevine base. The sprigs of cedar were attached first, followed by hydrangea blossoms. Then came a strand of pearl garland, available by the foot at craft shops; the designer wired one end to the base and looped it around the wreath, hotgluing it at strategic points. Dried pink roses, pepperberries, common backyard moss, and long, thin stalks of leptrosporum add color and shape.

Large, lush, and full, this wreath still looks light enough to hang above a delicate mantle. The base consists of branches of fresh bay leaves wired to an eight-inch (20 cm.) wire ring. Gold sleigh bells are wired onto the base between the leaves, and flowers and herbs are hot-glued at random: zinnias, boneset, strawflowers, artemisia, and unidentified pink berries from the designer's backyard.

Neon-yellow lemons contrast nicely with dark magnolia leaves. A straw base works well for this kind of wreath. To make a similar one, first pin magnolia leaves around the front, using floral pins, making sure the leaves point outward. Then fill in the front of the wreath with pine, attaching it with pins, and pick clusters of boxwood between the magnolia leaves. Now for the lemons. Pierce each one end-to-end with a piece of heavy (18-gauge) wire, leaving several inches protruding from each end. Fold the wire ends straight back, and push them through the base, front to back, tucking the ends into back of the base. Hot-glue heads of red yarrow onto the greenery, and add a few cone flowers.

Because this fresh fruit wreath is heavy, the designer made a double base. She cut out a wreath-shaped piece of thin plywood and hammered medium-small nails through the wood, back to front, encircling the base and leaving the sharp nails projecting from the front side. Then she pushed blocks of dry foam onto the nails, producing a foam base backed with wood—which she then covered with Spanish moss.

Magnolia leaves picked around the outside and inside diameters form the basic wreath shape, and fruit supplies the decoration. The grapes are attached with U-shaped wires inserted over the stems at strategic locations. The apples and oranges are impaled on picks, whose pointed ends are inserted into the foam. Cinnamon sticks are picked and hot-glued around for accents.

LEFT: Glittering copper ribbon and matte green leaves—contrasting colors and surfaces make this table wreath an intriguing centerpiece. The designer covered the straw base with protea leaves, picking them at an angle so that they overlap well. She then taped plastic candle holders onto the base. Next came wispy plumosa fern, hot-glued between the leaves. She gave the wreath two bows: first a large one of copper-foil ribbon, then a smaller one on top. Finally, she hot-glued white parchment flowers around the bow and inserted the candles.

BELOW: Supported by a well-soaked ring of wet foam, the materials in this fresh table wreath will last throughout the Christmas season. Evergreens are inserted directly into the foam, and weak-stemmed English ivy is picked in. The tangerines are wired onto the base. (To wire the fruit, pierce it from side to side with a piece of heavy floral wire, leaving about two inches on each side. Bend the ends straight back, and insert them into the foam.) Hot-glue cinnamon sticks to the ends of picks and insert into the foam.

A white wreath on a dark door—
what could be more striking? This
bunnytail wreath would impress
even the bunnies. To make it, you'll
need white and red bunnytails,
both available at craft shops. Wire
the white bunnytails into full
bunches, about four inches (10
cm.) wide and six inches (15 cm.)
long. Then wire the bunches to a
24-inch (60 cm.) wreath base—
either vine or wire will do—overlapping them so that the stems are covered. For a full, lush look, make
sure to cover the inside and outside
diameters, as well as the front. Wire
together small bunches of red bunnytails, attach to picks, and insert
them into the wreath at random.

Paint some tiny baskets gold
(these are one inch wide and two
inches high, or 2.5 by 5 cm.). Wire
a pick to the back of each basket,
and hot-glue a sprig of greenery
inside, at the back. Glue dried
roses, celosia, and globe amaranth
inside each basket, to make miniature arrangements. Pick in the baskets around the wreath.

Form a bow from gold wired-
net ribbon and wire it to the
wreath, arranging the streamers
around the wreath and wiring
them into position.

The two window arrangements
echo the wreath. The copper containers hang from ribbon and conceal bricks of foam. Each tiny, gold-
painted basket holds a sprig of boxwood glued to the inside back,
roses, and white ammobium
blooms. Hook one end of a piece
of wire through the bottom of the
basket; the other end will be inserted into the foam.

Insert small branches of Scotch
pine at the corners of the container.
Then add lots of red bunnytails
and a few white ones, some globe
amaranth, and thistles. Insert the
picked baskets and, toward the
back, stems of rice grass. Tie a
length of ribbon to the handles,
and hang.

ARRANGEMENTS

Materials and container echo each other in this coppery arrangement. A block of foam holds dried flowers and grasses, some common, some not (local crafts stores often carry surprising numbers of dried naturals).

Starting at the center back, insert stems of cinquefoil across the width of the container, spacing them evenly. Then add rows of natural bunnytails, peach rice grass, peach peppergrass, and baby's breath. Add peach statice sinuata in front, leaving a small space for the ornament. Attach a piece of wire to the top of the ornament, and insert it into the foam. Form a bow by wrapping wired metallic-copper ribbon around a candle, a dowel, or your finger; attach a wire, insert it into the foam, and position the streamers.

LEFT: Graceful lines and traditional Christmas colors characterize this striking arrangement. The designer began by cutting a piece of dry foam to fit a purchased pine-needle basket, and then covering the foam with deer moss. She attached slim red tapers to six-inch (15 cm.) picks with floral tape, and inserted them into the foam. Then came the vertical and horizonal cedar boughs, to establish the arrangement's basic shape, and the pine cones, attached to picks.

(Holes drilled in the cones made it easier to insert the picks.) Red rose hips and white rabbit tobacco added color, along with dried pomegranates cut in half and hot-glued to picks (one was hot-glued directly onto the front of the basket). An extra cone and a red bird were hot-glued to the bottom, and loops of watered-silk grosgrain ribbon picked in for a final touch.

BELOW: This Christmas mail-box is even busier than most.

Green velvet ribbons were hot-glued around the box, front and back, along with an alert-looking bird. Lined with plastic, the mail-box holds a water-soaked piece of wet floral foam, into which the designer inserted whatever green-ery was at hand. A streamer of ivy was pulled up across the box and tucked under the bird, to keep his feet warm. Berries and twigs were inserted into the foam, and various nuts, cones, and acorns hot-glued in place.

Orchids and onions, eucalyptus and okra—if you're more interested in shapes and colors than in traditional categories, you'll combine odd things, often with arresting results.

Centered in the whitewashed market basket is a bowl containing wet floral foam and held in place by crumpled newspaper. First came a base of greenery: cedar, silver dollar eucalyptus, and variegated foliage. Then came the fruit. The bunch of red grapes was wired at the stem, then wired around a large pick. Large picks were inserted directly into the other produce—red onions, mushrooms, and okra— and then into the foam. Last came the flowers, inserted directly into the foam: giant white fujimums, a stalk of fleshy green leucodendron in the center, and elegant orchids.

The sweeping lines and subtle colors of this arrangement earn it a place at any table. A gold-painted basket lined with heavy plastic acts as a container, with a water-soaked piece of floral foam taped inside. The first materials used were three large pieces of cedar, inserted to form a triangle. Then dried pomegranates and step mushrooms were picked in, emphasizing the triangular shape. A lamé tube bow provides the focal point, with additional pomegranates, mushrooms, and gold-painted sweet gum balls clustered around it. Two 20-inch (50 cm.) mauve candles were taped to wooden picks and inserted slightly to the right of center, with boxwood and more cedar used to fill in around the accent pieces.

Full, heavy sorghum tops can produce a lush arrangement. For this one, the designer cut a piece of dry foam to fit a rustic basket, and covered it with moss. Since the sorghum tops were the heaviest materials, she inserted them first, establishing the basic shape of the arrangement. Then came common field thistles, followed by dried red and pink roses. Branches of lunaria (money plant) added round white leaves, and red eucalyptus added burgundy ones. The final touches were sprigs of baby's breath and a velvet bow.

LEFT: Nothing warms the heart (and the feet) like a roaring fire, and these pine cones will set even the stubbornest logs ablaze. Coated in paraffin and scented with cinnamon oil, they can be tossed in the fireplace, covered with kindling and "squaw wood," and lit with a match, adding their flames to the fire and their fragrance to the house. Packed in an attractive basket and bedecked with a bow, these fire starters make a perfect gift for friends who love a fire but hate to build one.

The ingredients include pine cones of various sizes, paraffin (available at most hardware stores and wherever canning supplies are sold), a double boiler, red crayons, and cinnamon oil (one teaspoon to two pounds of paraffin).

Cover your work table with newspaper. Remove the paper from the crayons, and break them into pieces. Melt the paraffin in a double boiler over hot water. *Do not melt paraffin directly on the burner or over an open flame. It may catch fire if you do.* Add pieces of red crayon until the wax is the desired color, then add the cinnamon oil.

Using tongs, dip the pine cones in the paraffin, and set them on the newspaper to dry. Allow the coated cones to dry, and then dip them again; repeat until cones are well covered. Allow the wax to dry completely.

Like all flammable materials, the cones should be stored a safe distance from the fire.

BELOW: The toys and goodies in these sleighs are all natural materials, wired into the spray-painted wicker sides. The white sleigh contains sprigs of holly and evergreen, peppers, cinnamon sticks, nuts, Christmas cherry, and prickly brown burrs. Riding in the red sleigh are sprigs of evergreen, statice, strawflower, peppers, cinnamon sticks, nuts, and Christmas cherry.

This three-foot (90 cm.) candy cane won't hurt your teeth or your waistline; it was cut from a two-inch-thick (5 cm.) sheet of foam. Natural materials picked in careful rows create the striped illusion.

A background of Fraser fir alternates with rows of red and then pink globe amaranth, tufted celosia, and bushy heads of sedum Autumn Joy. Hang this wall arrangement in a prominent place, and enjoy all those admiring comments.

Like most stockings, this one is filled with nice surprises. The base is a piece of two-inch-thick foam (5 cm.) cut into the proper shape. Sprigs of ground pine were picked in for greenery, with two or three sprigs per pick. Spilling out of the top are branches of Fraser fir, German statice, pink amaranth, celosia, yarrow, sumac heads, and statice sinuata in bright pink and purple.

LEFT: This woodsy arrangement looks as if it came out of someone's backyard. It did—and a small backyard, at that. A natural stick basket lined with heavy plastic holds a brick of wet floral foam, lying catty-cornered, back left to front right. Moss tucked around the foam hides it from view. Mushrooms on floral picks were inserted into the foam through the sides of the basket, and a few lichen-covered twigs hot-glued to the outside. Various greenery was then inserted into the foam—mountain laurel, white pine, holly, hemlock, and some variegated shrubbery no one could identify. Ivy streamers trail out the sides and encircle the handle. A few gold-spray-painted sorghum heads add body, some nameless red berries add color, and a perky little bird, hot-glued to the handle, adds cheer.

BELOW: This little basket (6-1/2 inches, or 16.25 cm., tall), frosted with a gold paint pen, holds a variety of unusual materials, all hot-glued to the inside: boneset, love-in-a-mist pods, globe amaranth, strawflowers, and gilded boxwood sprigs. Narrow ribbon is woven through the center of a length of net ribbon, which is glued to the handle. A bow made from 3/4-inch (1.9 cm.) wired ribbon, complete with streamers, graces the front.

ORNAMENTS

LEFT: The miniature baskets sold in every craft store make perfect Christmas tree ornaments. Just hot-glue small sprigs of dried materials inside. These contain yarrow, German statice, peppergrass, baby's breath, and globe amaranth. The handles are decorated with three narrow ribbons braided together and tied in a small bow at the center. Hot glue secures the ribbon in the center and on the sides.

TOP RIGHT: This elaborate ornament would be at home on the most formal tree. To make a similar one, you'll need about five feet (1.5 m.) of 1/8-inch (3 mm.) ribbon in one color, 10 feet (3 m.) in another color (divided in half), and a yard (90 cm.) of tiny glass beads, along with a basket and some dried flowers.

First braid a 16-inch (40 cm.) strip, using two strips of ribbon and one of beads; knot and glue the ends. Braid the remaining ribbon, and glue it to the basket as shown. Then glue the beads next to the braided ribbon. Glue the flowers and greenery into the basket: celosia, German statice, and eucalyptus leaves. Glue any loose beads in the center of the eucalyptus leaves, and glue braided bead-and-ribbon strips at the sides, allowing the extra to hang down the sides.

BOTTOM RIGHT: The designer used three kinds of ribbon on this gold-sprayed basket: net, plain, and wired. She wrapped three-inch (7.5 cm.) net ribbon around the basket and 1/8-inch (3 mm.) gold ribbon around the handle; both were hot-glued at the ends. Then she hot-glued baby's breath, rosebuds, strawflowers, globe amaranth, boxwood sprigs, and rose hips inside. Finally, she glued a small wired-ribbon bow to the handle.

For even dressier baskets, spray-paint them gold and wrap them in lace, securing it with hot glue, as this designer did. Because the dried materials are very delicate, she filled the baskets with wet-style floral foam and covered it with Spanish moss. She wired several fragrant star anise and inserted them into the foam, then added lavender, tansy, statice sinuata, caspia, pearly everlasting, artemisia, crested celosia, euca-lyptus, and globe amaranth. Gold cord serves as hangers.

Touches of color warm the icy glitter of these icicles. Glued to the tops are tiny sprigs of asparagus fern, peppergrass, German statice, pepperberries, celosia, strawflowers, and an occasional rose. Ribbons serve as hangers.

Elongated ornaments are interesting contrasts to the usual round shapes that bedeck the tree. Glued to the blown-glass ornament at left are silver king artemisia, sprigs of blue salvia, and delphinium blooms. The ornament at right boasts German statice, tiny pink peppergrass, strawflowers, pepperberries, celosia, and globe amaranth. Each is topped with a ribbon that serves as a hanger.

Blown-glass bells cascading down the tree add both color and sound; they really do ring when a draft moves through the room. Hot-glued on top are German statice, pepperberries, celosia, peppergrass, and globe amaranth. Loops of ribbon make graceful hangers.

LEFT: Ordinary glass Christmas balls can become distinctive ornaments with natural materials hot-glued to the outside and a bright bow tied to the hanger. A well-shaped leaf of dusty miller adorns the silver ball at far left, topped with a sprig of blue salvia and a delphinium bloom. Silver ribbon ties it all together. The blown glass ornament at left also holds dusty miller, topped with artemisia and delphinium. The wired blue ribbon makes an especially effective bow.

The red and white bouquet in the inset photo consists of German statice, globe amaranth, and celosia.

TOP RIGHT: On these ornaments, dusty miller leaves support dainty peppergrass, topped with pepperberries and strawflowers. The materials at far right also include dusty miller, peppergrass, and strawflowers, but add celosia and a pink rose on top.

BOTTOM RIGHT: Glass balls filled with potpourri add scent to the tree. Remove the metal hook and wire from the top of the ornament, fill the ball about a third full of potpourri, and reattach hook to top, using a drop of quick glue. Run a piece of thin floral wire through a piece of lace, gathering it, and attach it to the top. Add a bow and hanger, and top bow with globe amaranth.

Miniature vine wreaths make versatile bases. You can buy them ready-made or make your own: just shape the vines into wreaths and tie or wire together. Then select herbs and everlastings in complementary colors and hot-glue them around the wreath in sequence.

Mountain mint was the first herb applied to these wreaths; the leaves cover the bases, overlapping in the same direction. Accent materials add color and shape: lavender, nigella, strawflowers, pearly everlasting, globe amaranth, crested celosia, and artemisia.

These wreath bases are wire and lace. To make one, thread a piece of floral wire though a piece of lace 15 inches (37.5 cm.) long and four inches (10 cm.) wide, gathering it by going in and out of the holes until you've formed a seven-inch (17.5 cm) circle. Tie the wire together, and add a ribbon loop as a hanger. Very carefully dot hot glue along the wire, fold the lace over, and hold until dry, doubling it for a fluffy effect. Hot-glue mountain mint leaves around the inside of the lace circle, and then hot-glue on your remaining herbs and flowers: sweet Annie for fragrance, crested celosia, globe amaranth, strawflowers, and pearly everlasting.

Strawberry corn is an ornamental with cobs about two inches (5 cm.) long. Available as seed corn for the home garden or as full-grown cobs in the fall, strawberry corn is a perfect shape and color for a Christmas ornament.

This cob was shorn of its husks, sprayed with a glossy acrylic coating, and allowed to dry. Five holly leaves painted gold (either paint pen or spray can would work) were hot-glued on top, along with a loop of gold wire with attached stars, to serve as a hanger. Finally, a small sprig of pepperberries was hot-glued on top.

The corn husks were left on this cob of strawberry corn, becoming essential parts of the design. After soaking for a few minutes in warm water, the brittle husks became pliable enough to work with. When dry, they were gilded with a paintbrush barely dipped in gold paint.

A loop of ribbon hot-glued to the center of the cob serves as a hanger. Most of the husk tips were bent forward and glued onto the corn, forming loops; two were left extended. Eucalyptus leaves were overlapped around the top of the cob, and celosia and globe amaranth filled in the spaces created by the loops. The tip of a eucalyptus branch was glued to the bottom of the ornament, to help balance it visually, and the ornament sprayed with a glossy acrylic finish.

LEFT: Red, white, and gold—these joyous colors are reflected in natural materials. The husks on the strawberry corn were soaked for a few minutes, to make them pliable, then trimmed with scissors into shorter and narrower shapes. When they were almost dry, they were bent into interesting shapes, then allowed to dry completely. With the cob covered in plastic wrap, for protection, the husks were spray-painted gold, top and bottom. A piece of gold cord was hot-glued on as a hanger. Then came the flowers. Glue was applied to the ends of white ammobium blossoms, and the flowers placed at random. Finally, the cob was sprayed with clear acrylic finish.

RIGHT: This zippy ornament consists of kernels of Indian corn glued onto a foam ball. A "hairpin" made of floral wire, looped and inserted into the ball, forms the hanger, and plaid ribbon in complementary colors provides a finishing touch.

LEFT: Pomanders are time-honored Christmas decorations, and for excellent reason. They're fragrant, pretty, and made from everyday materials. Pierce a whole fresh orange all over with a nail, and insert whole cloves into the holes. (The nail spares fingers and cloves.) Let the pomander dry until it feels almost weightless, compared to its former hefty self. Drying takes about six hours in a dehydrator and several days in a dry, cool place. Attach a ribbon as if wrapping a package and tie a knot on top, leaving the ends long enough to make a hanger. Hot-glue three bay leaves around the knot and three caspia on top. Then add one-inch (2.5 cm.) cinnamon sticks, strawflowers, and whole star anise. Finish with three globe amaranth, glued as close to the ribbon as possible. Tie the ribbon ends together as a hanger.

RIGHT: Both evergreen and cinnamon have distinctive Christmas scents. Together, they can infuse an entire house with holiday spirit.

Each of these fragrant ornaments consists of a purchased cinnamon broom decorated with herbs and flowers. A small bunch of naturals was wired together with fine-gauge floral wire, spread out into a fan shape to match the broom, and then wired onto the neck of the broom.

The brilliant broom at right supports magenta globe amaranth and small white snowflake flowers on a bed of garden thyme and silver king artemisia. The broom in the inset photo is decorated with silver king artemisia and yarrow, both natural yellow and dyed orange with fabric dye.

Fragrant spice balls become lovely tree decorations when dried leaves and flowers are added. A piece of lace was folded accordion-style, wired in a circle, and hot-glued to the top of the ball. Then leaves and flowers were hot-glued to the lace. While the lace isn't a prominent feature of the ornament, it does provide an attractive base.

LEFT: The ornament at top is decorated with silver-green lamb's ears, yellow tansy, fuzzy stillingia, and a rosebud. The lower spice ball sports peppermint leaves and flowers, and colorful globe amaranth.

BELOW: The left and center spice balls are enlivened with German statice, loops of metallic ribbon, and a prominent rose. The ball at right adds silver germander leaves to the mix.

Making Spice Balls

These small pomanders are really highly spiced applesauce. To make them, drain a jar of applesauce for about 30 minutes. In a medium mixing bowl, combine ground cinnamon, cloves, mace, and nutmeg in equal amounts. Gradually add drained applesauce to the spices until the mixture has the consistency of stiff cookie dough. Shape the dough into balls, place them on waxed paper, and allow to dry for three weeks (longer in humid weather). Decorate the spice balls with ribbons, lace, and dried materials.

LEFT: Most of us have spent a cozy December evening stringing popcorn and cranberries for the Christmas tree. Dried flowers—in this case, globe amaranth—can be strung in exactly the same way for a brilliant and unusual garland. Remove the stems but keep the leaves that are inclined to remain. Then thread a large needle with thin monofilament (fishing line) or heavy thread, and string the flowers. When the garland is the length you want (or when you run out of flowers), tie off both ends, and drape the garland through the branches.

RIGHT: Scatter small nosegays of dried flowers through the branches of your tree, for a pretty, light-hearted effect. Just wrap some floral wire about the stems, leaving enough excess wire to form a loop at the bottom; the loop will wrap around the tree branch, holding the nosegay in place. Then wrap the stems with floral tape, to create a smooth, firm handle.

The nosegay on top consists of sage, statice sinuata, German statice, and magenta globe amaranth. The one at center left boasts red and white strawflowers, pearly everlasting, and red and pink amaranth. At center right is a nosegay of red celosia, white statice sinuata, and pink and white amaranth. The simple white ornament at bottom contains pearly everlasting, silver king artemisia, and white amaranth.

LEFT: If you've been wondering what to do with the seashells you gathered last summer, here's one solution. Loosely fold a length of ribbon in half and hot-glue it to the back of the shell, so that a loop about an inch (2.5 cm.) long shows on top and tails of about two inches (5 cm.) show on the bottom. Hot-glue herbs and flowers to the front side: mint leaves in a triangle, overlaid with caspia, then lavender, celosia, strawflowers, and tiny globe amaranth.

RIGHT: They may look elaborate, but these miniature tussie mussies are simply tiny bouquets in small paper-doily cuffs, available at most crafts stores. Start by gluing shapely green leaves (these are mint) around the base. Then make a small bouquet of dried flowers and herbs, wrapping the stems together with floral tape, positioning the flowers on the outside lower than those in the center. (Don't let the bouquet get too wide to fit into the cuff.) Cut the stems to two or three inches (5 to 7.5 cm.), and insert the stems into the cuff. Rewrap with tape to secure cuff. Add a bow of gold curling-paper ribbon and a hanger of gold elastic cord.

The bouquets shown include roses, sweet Annie, lavender, statice sinuata, pearly everlasting, and globe amaranth.

LEFT: Scented geranium leaves, catnip flowers, roses, lavender, straw-flowers, globe amaranth, celosia, statice sinuata, artemisia—all grace this Victorian ornament. If your favorite craft store doesn't stock paper cones rimmed with lace, cut a paper disc, make a cut from the outside edge to the center, and glue the cone together. Snip off the point and glue a piece of lace around the top. Fold two eight-inch (20 cm.) pieces of ribbon in half, wire them in the center, and insert them through the hole at the bottom, leaving enough inside the cone to hot-glue in place. Hot-glue a ribbon hanger to the rim, a piece of floral foam inside the cone, and green forest moss over it. Working from the perimeter to the center and leaving a rim of moss showing, hot-glue herbs and flowers on the moss. Add a small dove.

TOP: "What on earth is *that?*" will break the ice rather well at your Christmas open house—a good reason to deck your tree with exotic lotus pods, available in the "drieds" section of the local craft store. Spray-paint the pod gold, and drill a hole into the stalk end. Fold a length of gold cord in half and hot-glue both ends in the hole, to serve as a hanger. Then hot-glue on herbs, flowers and a small bird.

BOTTOM: According to Scandinavian legend, each bird on your Christmas tree will bring one year of good luck. Start your aviary with a bluebird nesting in potpourri. Run a wire up through the bottom of a purchased nest and back out again, to wrap around a tree branch. Apply hot glue to the inside of the nest and spread with potpourri. Install the bird with hot glue, and surround him or her with herbs and flowers.

Each of these intricate ornaments is a circle of red cardboard with seeds arranged in an interesting pattern, attached with white craft glue. At left, sea oats form a backdrop for white squash seeds, brown persimmon seeds, cantaloupe seeds dyed green, and a hemlock cone. The center ornament includes sea oats, corn kernels, hemlock cones, cantaloupe seeds dyed blue, and a eucalyptus pod. At right, the sea oats are topped with cantaloupe seeds dyed red, Job's tears, Japanese watermelon seeds, and a small cone cup.

To make a double ornament that can be displayed from both sides, make two and glue them back to back.

The bells of Christmas are ringing! To make these bright ornaments, cut a bell shape from cardboard and from two pieces of felt. Glue the three together, using white craft glue, with the cardboard in the middle to add stiffness. Then glue on some seeds or small cones.

The red bell is decorated with squash seeds and a small acorn in the center. The blue bell adds some variegated Japanese watermelon seeds. On the green bell are sea oats, hemlock cones, cantaloupe seeds dyed red, and a small acorn in the center.

How to Dye Seeds
Wash any pulp from the seeds, and allow them to dry thoroughly. Spread them out on a baking sheet and set them in a sunny place or in a warm oven until they are thoroughly dry.

Combine one tablespoon of ordinary fabric dye, two cups of water, and a little salt in an enamel pan. For a deeper color, add more dye. Boil the seeds until you like the color, then set them aside to dry.

LEFT: Sweet or hot, red peppers are colorful enough to hang on the tree. The large ancho peppers are tied by their stems with bright red raffia and decked out in nuts, cones and eucalyptus—all hot-glued in place. Bright raffia bows add pizzazz.

The small rings were made by threading fruit and nuts onto a piece of medium-gauge floral wire, then forming the wire into a circle and hooking the ends around each other, so that the circle stays closed. The upper ornament holds nuts, hot peppers, and Christmas cherries. The lower one adds two orange calendula blossoms.

TOP RIGHT: Pine cones can be had for the picking. Make sure the cones are firm, then hot-glue the ends of a red velvet ribbon to the underside of a couple of the cone's seeds. Finally, hot-glue your materials in place: cedar, rose hips, and a bright red bow.

BOTTOM RIGHT: Star-shaped cotton bolls can be decorated as rustic-looking ornaments. The top one has a seed "daisy" with a gumball center and petals made from cherry pits and pumpkin seeds. The bottom boll is dressed with a small gumball and hemlock cones. Both hang from red velvet ribbons hot-glued in place.

Christmas in the kitchen doesn't have to stop with once-a-year cookies and cranberries. Everyday garlic, that fragrant herb we couldn't do without, deserves a little finery too. Hot-glue some rosemary sprigs and scarlet globe amaranth among the bulbs of a garlic swag, attach a bow made from wired-cord ribbon, and hang the swag where you can admire it—and where it will keep the Christmas vampires at bay.

LEFT: This six-foot (1.8 m.) garland is just the right length to dress up a plain white door. It displays four different shades of green because it's made from four different evergreens: hemlock, white pine, blue juniper, and evergreen japonica. Rabbit tobacco lightens the garland with touches of white. The ingredients were wired separately into bundles with fine-gauge floral wire, and the bundles wired to a spine of heavy-gauge wire. A six-foot garland requires about 40 sprigs of each evergreen and as many bundles of flowers as you like.

RIGHT: There's nothing complex about this festive swag: branches of evergreens and holly arranged in a fan shape and wired together at the top, with a red velvet bow wired on for color. For easier hanging, make a loop of wire and attach it before adding the bow.

These swags are simply horizontal bouquets held together with wire and hot glue. The base of the green and red swag is a large bunch of eucalyptus and silver king artemisia, wired together in the middle. Pepperberries and cranberry celosia are hot-glued to the base, and a paper bow is wired to the center.

The smaller pink swag has a base of silver king artemisia, wired in the center, with other materials hot-glued on top: long pink larkspur, crested celosia, hydrangea, and strawflowers. A bow of pink grosgrain ribbon ties the colors together.

The materials for this festive garland are as simple as the technique used to make it. A length of green jute cord (the type used in macrame) was stretched taut between two chair backs, at a comfortable working height. Then bunches of pine and gypsophila (baby's breath) were alternately tied to the cord with flexible, spool-type floral wire, each bunch overlapping the previous one. Bright plaid bows were wired to the ends.

Many craft stores carry wheat sheaves that are wired, fumigated, and ready for decorating. If you gather wheat from the fields, zap it for a few seconds in the microwave or fumigate it, to get rid of bugs. Then shape it into a sheaf and wire it together around the middle. Trim off some of the wheat heads on one side, so that the swag will hang flat against the wall. (Save the trimmings.) Make six bows with three loops on each side (you don't need a center loop), wire each in the center, and wire the bows tightly to the sheaf. Hot-glue the trimmed wheat heads randomly among the ribbons. If you hang your sheaf outside, like the one in the inset photo, prepare to fend off hungry birds.

You can dress up a cabinet of collectibles with Christmas candles, fresh fruit, and a graceful garland. Or, in this case, three garlands: cedar, cranberry, and ivy. You'll need small nails on the top of the cabinet—in the center and at both corners—to hold the garland, or some other means of attachment.

First make a cedar garland. Wire small bunches of cedar along a piece of five-ply jute cord, overlapping the bunches for fullness and to conceal the previous wired ends.

Now string very fresh cranberries on lengths of substantial thread, with buttons at the beginning and end to keep the cranberries in place.

Finally, wire together lengths of ivy to make a garland. Twist the ivy and berry garlands around each other, and tie with string every 12 inches (30 cm.) or so.

Wire the cedar garland to the center nail, then to the two outer ones, allowing it to droop gracefully in between. Wire the berry-ivy garland to the center nail and then to the outer ones, allowing it to drape down the sides of the cabinet.

Form a bow, wire it to the center nail, arrange the streamers the way you want them, and wire into position. Wire on some holly leaves, novelty packages, sumac heads, or anything else you have around that would look good. Finally, arrange cedar branches, fruit, and candles at the base.

LEFT: This handsome door swag is too heavy to rely on foam alone for support. The designer hot-glued a long rectangle of two-inch-thick green Styrofoam (5 cm.) to a sturdy board; the foam provided a means of anchoring the greenery, and the board supplied the necessary backing.

After he built the support, the designer secured a brass trumpet to the foam with an electrical conduit clamp. Branches of Fraser fir, picked into the foam, established the general shape. Then he filled in the center with short pieces of fir, eucalyptus, and boxwood. Dried pomegranates, cones, celosia, and wheat, picked in bunches, add interesting detail, along with a bow and streamers of Hunter green grosgrain ribbon.

A single cinnamon broom can fill a house—a large house—with the sweet, spicy scent that says Christmas. Widely available, the brooms can be decorated with just about anything. For this one, the designer wired on some cattails first and some corn husk flowers second, twisting the flower stems through the broom and adding more wire in back. (To make the flowers, see page 23.) She then made six plaid bows with three loops on each side and wired them over the cattails and around the flowers.

BELOW: For this glitzy swag, the designer spray-painted two bunches of wheat a bright silver, laid them end-to-end, and wired them together by their stems. After hot-gluing on some sprigs of peppergrass, she covered the wire with ribbon, then hot-glued a bow to the front and a pink-painted sea grape leaf to the back.

RIGHT: Old hand tools are often pleasing to the eye. With more work to do than time to do it in, our ancestors honed and shaped and experimented, searching for the most efficient design, the most muscle-sparing shape. As often as not, efficiency and grace went together. The owner of this antique sickle wired a period-looking bow to it, hot-glued pine and eucalyptus sprigs under the bow, hot-glued on some dried caspia, and hung the attention-getting swag on the wall.

Trees & Topiaries

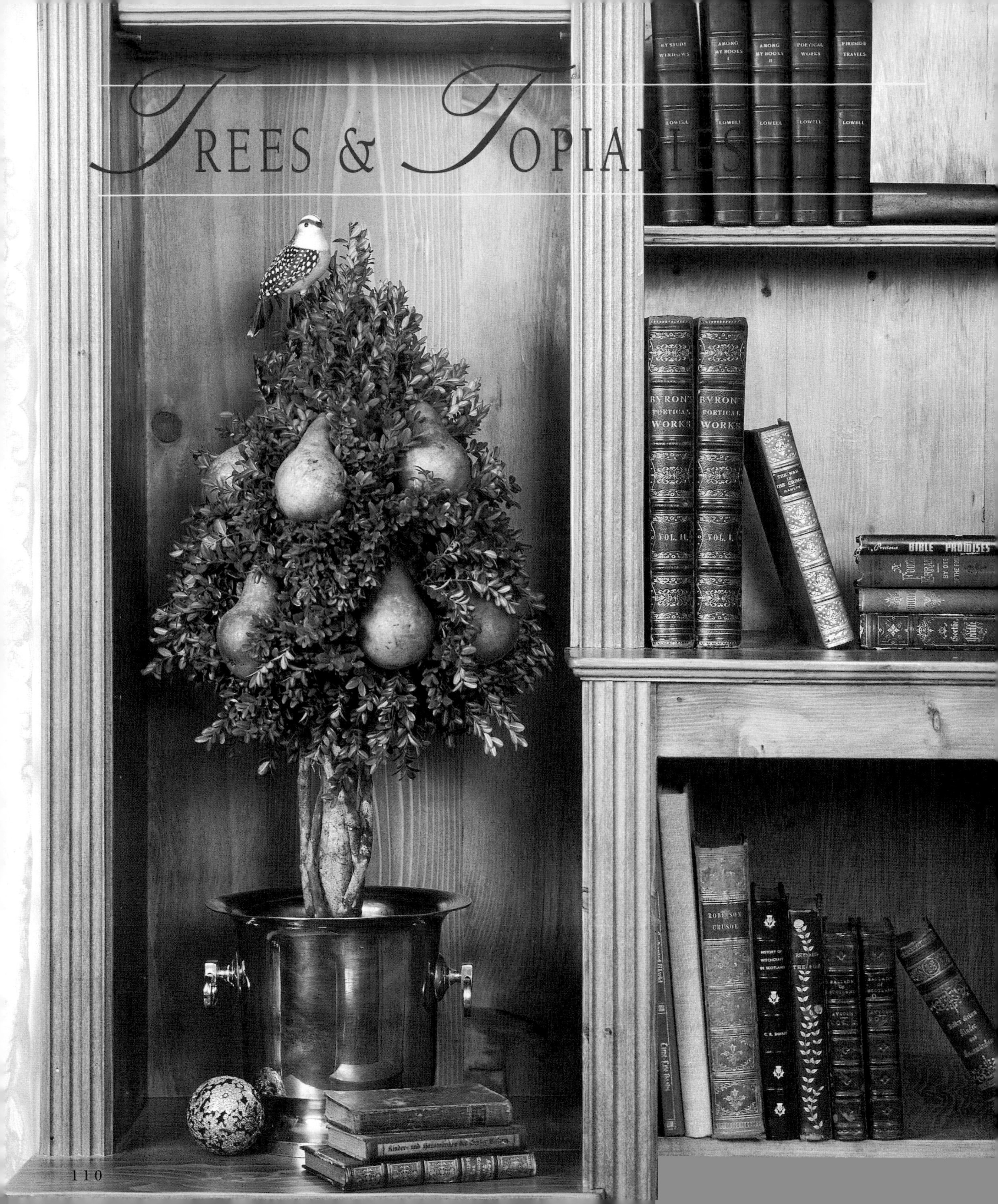

LEFT: A partridge in a pear tree can perch happily on buffet table or bookcase. Inside the brass container, a green plastic pot full of plaster of Paris holds a tree branch upright and steady. The top of the plaster is spray-painted moss green, for camouflage. A foam cone, hot-glued to the top of the "trunk," holds sprigs of boxwood inserted at a downward slope. (In this case, the designer began at the top and continued downward to the base.) Strong-stemmed bosc pears are wired to three-inch (7.5 cm.) picks and inserted into the foam, and a purchased partridge roosts on top.

THIS PAGE: Flat but emphatically three-dimensional, this two-foot-tall (60 cm.) wall tree supplies that indispensable Christmas-tree fragrance. The base is a sheet of two-inch-thick (5 cm.) plastic foam cut in a tree shape. Pieces of Fraser fir are inserted at a sharp, downward-sloping angle, to mimic tree branches. Sumac heads and sprigs of German statice, both picked into the base, provide the red and white decorations.

A curly willow "trunk" makes this topiary as graceful as it is festive. After gluing dry foam into a clay pot and covering the foam with moss, the designer inserted the willow branches, their stems cut at a sharp angle for easier insertion. She then placed a foam ball in the top branches, tied the branches around the ball, and covered it with moss. Architecture completed, she turned to decorating. At top and bottom she picked evergreens, holly, and dried sweet Annie into the foam. Next she glued a length of ribbon to the top, wound it down to the bottom, and ended with a ribbon loop. Finally, she hot-glued on the apples, birds, and a bird's nest— which she also trimmed for Christmas.

This graceful topiary is simpler than it looks. To make a similar one, arrange a double handful of cattails around a sturdy dowel, then wire them in the middle and at the bottom. Wire on the upper bow, and cover its wire (and the one binding the cattails) with ribbon. Hot-glue pieces of fungus and sponge mushrooms to the base, glue on the lower bow, and tuck in some strands of Spanish moss. Finally, hot-glue sprigs of boxwood around the bows.

A grapevine tree is a woodsy base for materials straight from the forest. (For instructions on making one, see page 20.) This tree is lit with 35 clear mini-lights; the cord spirals down the inside of the tree, with the bulbs pulled through to the outside. A circle of plastic foam covered with sheet moss sits inside the bottom of the tree and holds two small pots of English ivy, whose streamers have been pulled out through the vines. Other materials are hot-glued directly onto the tree: dried mushrooms and lichens, deer moss, rabbit tobacco, dried sweetheart roses, hemlock cones, protea buds, and faux blackberries. Three feet (90 cm.) of gold bullion—a spiderweb-like gold thread—wraps around the tree as a garland.

Fresh carnations add color and a spicy scent to this tabletop tree. To build a similar one, stand a block of wet floral foam on end in the middle of a low serving dish (this one is 14 inches, or 35 cm., across), and tape the foam to the dish. Insert sprigs of boxwood, forming a tree shape. Then insert red sumac heads, spacing them equally around the tree, using the larger ones at the bottom. Add miniature pink carnations, again distributing them evenly. Then pick in German statice, white pine cone "roses" (cones cut in half), and gold-painted gumballs from a sweet gum tree. Water the tree daily, pouring water gently on top of the foam.

LEFT: This tree could not be simpler. Just trim a live, upright rosemary plant into a Christmas tree shape, and decorate it. This one is decorated with a miniature garland, tiny ornaments hung from gold thread, and stemless globe amaranth placed in the branches.

RIGHT: This shaggy little tree will endear itself to children visiting for the holidays. Put it in the guest bedroom you've assigned to the kids. A 12-inch (30 cm.) foam cone supports overlapping sprigs of white pine that have been inserted at an angle, allowing the needles to slope downward, like those of a real tree. A few sprigs were then inserted upright, at the top. The "ornaments" consist of statice, yarrow, sweet Annie, ambrosia, and silver king artemisia.

LEFT: Some years, December seems to be six weeks long, with enough time for everything we want to do. Other years, December has six days—max. If this is one of your short seasons, consider the advantages of an artificial tabletop tree. The base is ready-made, requiring at most a little trimming of extra-long branches. With enough natural materials, no one will ever know what it's like deep down.

This tree boasts a garland of blue larkspur glued end-to-end and spiraled down the tree. Gypsophila has been randomly scattered among the branches (a dab of hot glue on the cut stem holds each in place). Blue salvia hangs from the tips of the branches, held firmly by hot glue. Hot-glued globe amaranth blossoms cover the salvia ends and enliven other branches as well. A bow of wired ribbon tops the tree.

RIGHT: The contrasting colors in this free-standing tree are all supplied by natural materials. Ground pine and German statice contribute the green and white. Red is provided by celosia, purple by sage blossoms, and magenta by globe amaranth. All are picked into a 12-inch (30 cm.) foam cone.

The trees on both these pages started off green and artificial. On this page, a garland of naturals steals the show. To create a similar effect, twist Spanish moss into a "rope" and spiral it up the tree. Then, starting at the bottom, hot-glue flowers to the moss—in this case, roses, hydrangea, pearly everlasting, larkspur, celosia, peppergrass, strawflowers, statice, pepperberries, and globe amaranth. Cover the wooden stand with a piece of lace and a bow, and set another bow on top, with a small cluster of flowers hot-glued in the center.

Artemisia and German statice turned this faux green tree into a naturally pink-and-white one. The designer inserted small branches of both plants all over the tree, cementing them in place with hot glue. Decorative accents include small blown glass balls, larkspur, pearly everlasting, peppergrass, celosia, and strawflowers. A small bow with a rosebud in the center tops the tree, and gathered lace trim finishes the bottom.

PACKAGES

LEFT: The recipient of this gift will be at least as pleased by the decoration as by what's inside. The rich-looking paper has color enough, so the designer focused on scent and texture instead. Fir sprigs and boxwood hot-glued to the paper form a dark base, with pine cones and peppergrass glued on top.

BELOW: The deep green paper is a perfect backdrop for pale flowers and dark cones. Hot-glued to the paper in a cresent shape are pine cones, cone flowers (made by cutting the cones in half), German statice, pearly everlasting, and white strawflowers. One cone is lightly dusted with white spray paint.

LEFT: One of the best trends in gift-wrapping is the appearance of festive tote bags. They range in size from substantial to minuscule, ready to hold a VCR or a single truffle. This one is even more attractive than most. A corsage made of dried roses, pink-dyed peppergrass, sprays of pepperberries, and sprigs of boxwood is hot-glued to the bag.

BELOW: Wrapped in pink moiré paper, this elegant package will shine under the tree. A silver bow forms the center of the decoration, with materials hot-glued on each side: artemisia, dusty miller, celosia, dyed German statice, dyed peppergrass, and bunches of della robia grapes.

LEFT: This pink metallic bow is wired and ready to turn a mundane package into an occasion. The bow requires four feet (1.2 m.) of 1-1/2"-wide (3.75 cm.) ribbon. Leaving one tail 11 inches (27.5 cm) long and the other 19 inches (47.5 cm.) long, form a bow with six loops (three on each side) and wire it in the center, after pulling the tails into place. Leave enough wire to attach to a package's ribbon. Cut a disc of clear, lightweight plastic (check the kitchen) and glue it to the front of the bow, to serve as a base for the naturals. Working from the outside to the center, hot-glue the herbs and flowers onto the plastic disc: bay leaves, caspia, yarrow, lavender, statice, celosia, thistle, globe amaranth, and strawflowers.

CENTER: The square red package is decorated with pine cones, cinnamon sticks, star anise, and boxwood, hot-glued to the paper.

RIGHT: The elongated blooms of rattail celosia are the attention-getters on this small package. Also hot-glued to the pink moiré paper are boxwood, dyed peppergrass, and della robia fruit.

Acrylic paints and a cotton ball can turn a home-grown gourd into a portly Santa. Give the gourd time to dry—preferably several months—then wash it in a bleach-and-water solution, to remove the natural molds that grow during drying, and let dry for a few more days. Sketch the Santa's outlines and paint, starting with the large expanses of color and finishing with the fine details. When the paints are dry, spray the gourd with acrylic sealer and glue on the cotton.

BIBLIOGRAPHY

Cusick, Dawn. *A Scented Christmas.* New York: Sterling Publishing Company, 1990.

Cusick, Dawn, and Rob Pulleyn. *Wreaths 'Round the Year.* New York: Sterling Publishing Company, 1990.

Pulleyn, Rob. *The Wreath Book.* New York: Sterling Publishing Company, 1988.

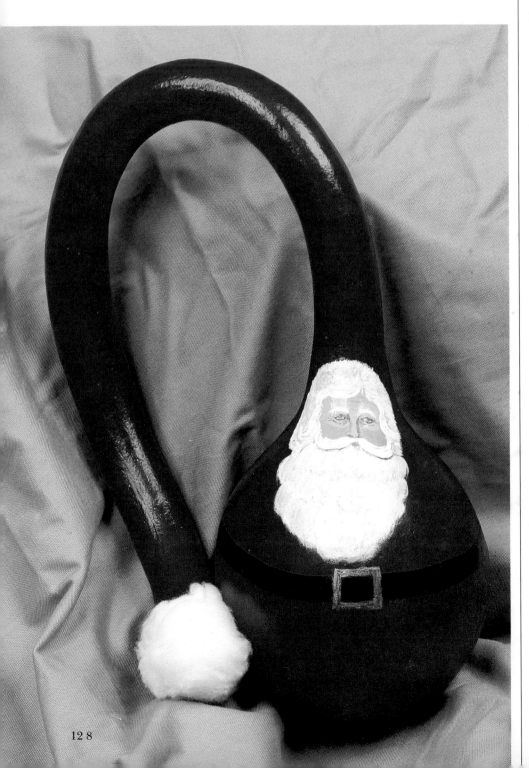